# A

## PRECIOUS MOMENTS™

### CHRISTMAS

Given to _____

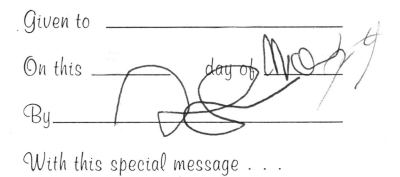

On this _____ day of _____

By _____

With this special message . . .

_____

_____

_____

# A

# CHRISTMAS

Published in Nashville, Tennessee, by Thomas Nelson, Inc., and distributed in Canada by Lawson Falle, Ltd., Cambridge, Ontario

Printed in the United States of America.
ISBN: 0-8407-7072-3

A
*Precious Moments*™

CHRISTMAS

BY

SAM BUTCHER

THOMAS NELSON PUBLISHERS
Nashville

Christmas is a time
for bows

And jingle bells
and winter snows . . .

Of holly wreaths
and colored lights

That twinkle
in the snowy nights.

Christmas is
a time for cakes

And other things
that Mommy makes . . .

Of little stockings
on the wall

With tiny treasures
in them all.

Christmas is a time
of joy

For every
little girl and boy . . .

A time of toys
and balls and bats

And puppy dogs
and baseball hats.

But just remember
Christmas brings

Much more than
toys and other things . . .

More than tinsel,
more than lights,

More than jingle bells
and snowy nights.

Most of all,
this time of year . . .

With all its love
and Christmas cheer . . .

Reminds us of
the gift of love

That came to us
from up above.

For long ago
in Bethlehem

A star arose
above the land.

Little angels
came to earth

To sing the news
of Jesus' birth.

The shepherds heard
their song of joy

And went to see
the baby boy.

Wisemen saw
his wondrous star

And made their
journey from afar.

They brought him
gifts of spice and gold

That Christmas day
so long foretold.

Now Christmas is
a time to share

The love of Jesus
everywhere . . .

A time when we
can laugh and sing

And thank the Lord
for everything.

So when you think
of snowy nights

With sleigh bells, trees,
and Christmas lights . . .

Above all else
remember, too,

God sent his gift
of love for you.

Merry Christmas!

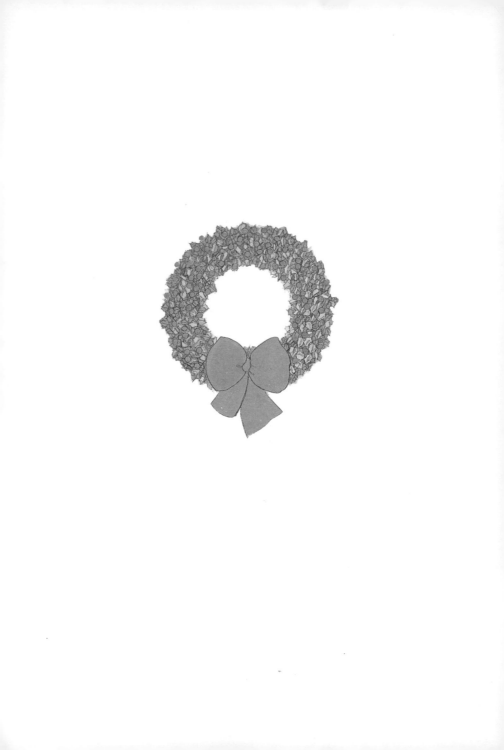